Consecrated to God

Other Andrew Murray titles:

Your Will Be Done
Prayer's Inner Chamber
The Coming Revival
The Cross of Christ
An Apostle's Inner Life
Working for God
The Ministry of Intercession
The Full Blessings of Pentecost
The Blood of the Cross
Waiting on God
Absolute Surrender
Humility
Abide in Christ
The Prayer Life
Christ is All
The Reign of Love
The Promise of the Spirit

Consecrated to God

ANDREW MURRAY

Edited by Simon Fox

Collins

Marshall Pickering

First published in 1990 by Marshall Pickering

Marshall Pickering is an imprint of the Collins
Religious Division, part of the Collins Publishing
Group, 8 Grafton Street, London W1X 3LA

Copyright © 1990 Marshall Pickering

All rights reserved. No part of this publication may be
reproduced, stored in a retrieval system, or transmitted,
in any form or by any means, electronic, mechanical,
photocopying, recording or otherwise, without the
permission in writing of the publisher.

ISBN 0 720 80750 6

Text set in Times by Avocet Robinson, Buckingham.
Printed in Great Britain by Cox & Wyman, Reading,
Berks.

CONTENTS

1:	Consecration	1
2:	Surrendering to God's Will	12
3:	Consecration and Money	25
4:	Perfect in Christ	34
5:	Perfect in All the Will of God	37
6:	Not Perfected, Yet Perfect	41
7:	The Divine Standard	47
8:	Jesus, the Model of Perfection	51
9:	May the God of Peace Perfect You	54
10:	Perfected by God Himself	58
11:	Keeping Christ's Word	62
12:	To Love as Christ Loved	66
13:	God Living in Us	70
14:	The Likeness of Christ	74
15:	Waiting for God	78
16:	Humility, the Glory of the Creature	81
17:	A New Year Meditation	85

Chapter 1

Consecration

But who am I, and what is my people, that we should be able to offer so willingly after this sort? For all things come of thee, and of thine own have we given thee.

(1 Chronicles 29:14)

At the beginning of this chapter we read that David called the Israelite people and princes together and told them what materials he had prepared for the building of the Temple. He had also given some of his personal treasures of gold and silver. 'I have set my affection to the house of my God,' he explained (verses 3–5). And then he called upon the people for their personal gifts: 'Who then is willing to consecrate his service this day unto the Lord?' (5). In response to this they gave their offerings very willingly and joyfully. Then we read:

Wherefore David blessed the Lord before all the congregation: and David said, 'Blessed be thou, Lord God of Israel our father, for ever and ever. Thine, O Lord, is the greatness, and the power, and the glory, and the victory, and the majesty: for all that is in the heaven and in the earth is thine; thine is the kingdom, O Lord, and thou art exalted as head above all. Both riches and honour come of thee, and thou reignest over all; and in thine hand is power and might; and in thine hand it is to make great, and to give strength unto all. Now, therefore, our God, we thank thee, and praise thy glorious name. But who am I, and what is my people, that we should be able to offer so willingly after this sort? For all things come of thee, and of thine own have we given thee.

(verses 1–14)

One morning a few years ago I received the tragic news that four students from a college at which I sometimes preached had been drowned while out on a picnic. A large party had left the college one day to go up into the nearby mountains. The weather was beautiful to start with, but later a mist suddenly descended, and there was some heavy rainfall. Some of the students reached home safely, after a delay. But some others were cut off by the rushing waters of a swollen river. A young lady became trapped in the middle of the river and was swept away. Three young men were also lost. Less than two months before all four of them had heard me preach upon the very verses quoted above. I had asked them if they were willing to consecrate themselves to the Lord. The young lady had made a very clear

Consecration

response, one of the young men had felt called to study for the ministry, and the other two had joined the Christian Endeavour organisation. Dear friends, you are reading these words now; who knows what may happen to you tomorrow? May God give us all grace to consecrate ourselves to him and serve him as those who have only one day at a time to live.

I want us to think about what consecration means. The Lord Jesus thought the heathen world was worth so much that he gave his blood for it. Would you give your blood to save the heathen? God's word assures us that if we give our lives for them, if we set our hearts upon them, if we give ourselves up to pray for them, to think about them, to work for them by stirring up interest among others, if we give to missionary work or go to the mission field ourselves, God in heaven will use us and bless us. Dear friends, are you living to the utmost for what Jesus lived for – the salvation of men? But I do not wish to merely turn your thoughts to the heathen world and its needs; I want to turn you to the living Christ. I want to ask you to consider what the unsaved are worth to God the Father, and to the One who died to bring them back to God. May God give you and me the grace to get a clearer understanding of consecration, and may we come one step closer to the blessed God to whom we belong.

In his prayer David expresses his astonishment that God should allow the people to give back to him what is in fact his own: 'All things come of thee, and of thine own have we given thee.' It is a mystery that we are able to offer anything to God. Consecration is a miracle of grace. Four very precious thoughts are suggested by David's words:

1. God is the Owner of everything and he gives everything to us.
2. We have nothing except what we receive — but we may receive from God everything that we need.
3. It is our privilege and honour to give back to God what we receive from him.
4. God has a double joy when he receives back from us what he has given us.

If we can apply these thoughts to our lives — to our wealth, to our property, to our whole being with all its powers — we will then understand what consecration ought to be.

God the Giver

God is the Owner of everything. There is no power, wealth, goodness or love that does not come from him. This is the first step in consecration: understanding that all I have has been given to me by God. I must learn to believe in God as the great Owner and Giver of everything. I need to hold on to that truth. I have nothing that does not in reality belong to God. People may say, 'The money in my purse is mine,' but in fact it is God's. All things are his and his alone.

And yet it is the glory of God, and his very nature, to be always *giving*. It is his nature that he does not live for himself but for his creatures. His is a love which always delights in giving. Oh, this is a precious thought: *there is nothing that God has that he does not want to give!*

When God asks you for anything, he first gives it to you himself. Never be afraid about what God will ask of you; he only asks for what is his own, for what he has already given you. The Possessor, Owner and Giver of everything – this is our God! You can apply that truth to yourself, to your powers, to all you are and have. Study it, believe it and live in it every day, every hour, every moment.

Man the receiver

Just as it is the nature and glory of God to be always giving, *so it is the nature and glory of man to be always receiving*. What has God made us for? Each of us has been made to be a vessel into which God can pour out his life, his beauty, his happiness, his love. We are created to be receptacles and reservoirs of divine, heavenly life and blessing, filled with just as much of God's goodness as he can put into us. Have we understood that our true purpose, the object of our creation, is to be always receiving?

If we fully enter into this truth, it will teach us some precious lessons. First, it will show us the utter folly of being proud or conceited. How absurd! If I were to borrow a very fine suit and walk around boasting about it as if it were my own, people would say, 'What a fool!' It is the Everlasting God who owns everything we have; shall we dare to exalt ourselves on account of what is in reality all his?

Secondly, this great truth will teach us a valuable lesson about what our true position is. It is God's nature to be always giving, mine to be always receiving. Just as the lock and key fit each other, so God the Giver and I the receiver fit into each other. Often we worry ourselves about our needs, instead of going back to the root of all things and saying, 'Lord, I only want to be the receptacle of what the will of God means for me, of the power and the gifts and the love and the Spirit of God.' What could be more simple? We must come to God as receptacles — cleansed, emptied and humble. Come to him, and then God will delight in giving you all you need.

If I may with reverence say it, God cannot help himself; it is his promise and his nature to give. Blessing is always flowing out of him. You know how water always flows into the lowest places. If we will just be emptied and low, nothing but receptacles, what a blessed life we will live! Day by day we will praise him — 'You give and I accept, you bestow and I rejoice in receiving.' On a sunny day people open all their windows and enjoy the warmth and cheerfulness of the sunshine. May our hearts learn to be open, always drinking in the light and sunshine of God's love.

Giving to God

If God gives everything and I receive everything, then what comes next is very clear: *I must give everything back to God again*. What a privilege this is! Just so that we might be able to express our love and gratitude to the Lord and so that we might have the happiness of pleasing and serving him, the Everlasting God says to us, 'Come now, and give back to me all that I have given you.'

Consecration

And yet people say, 'Oh, but must I give everything back?' Brother, don't you know that there is no true happiness or blessedness except in giving to God? David knew this to be true. He said, 'Lord, what an unspeakable privilege it is for us to be allowed to give back to you what is your own!' We are doubly blessed because not only can we receive, but we can also in love render back to God what he gives us. People say, 'But doesn't God give us all these good gifts so that we can enjoy them?' But the reality of that enjoyment is in giving back.

Just think of Jesus. God gave him a wonderful body. He kept it holy and gave it as a sacrifice to God. That is the beauty of having a body. God has also given you a soul. The beauty of having a soul is in being able to give it back to God. People talk about the difficulties which having a strong will causes them. But one never can have too strong a will. The problem is that we do not give that strong will up to God as a vessel into which he can and will pour his Spirit, in order to enable it to do him splendid service.

We have now considered three thoughts: God gives everything; I receive everything; I give everything back to God. Will you aim to live in the light of these truths? Will you say in your heart, 'My God, teach me to give up everything to you'? Take your mind, with all its powers of thought, your tongue, with all its power of speaking, your heart, with all its affections, your property, your gold and silver, your everything – and lay it all at God's feet and say, 'Here is the covenant between you and me. You delight in giving me everything, and I delight in giving it all back to you.'

May God teach us to do that. If we could learn this simple lesson, there would be an end to so much of our difficulty in finding out the will of God, an end to all our holding back. Written across our hearts would be the resolve, 'God can do with me what he pleases. I belong to him, and all I have belongs to him.' Instead of always saying to God, 'Give, give, give,' we would say, 'Yes, Lord, you *do* give, you *do* love to give, and I love to give back to you.' I encourage you to live a life like that, and to discover that it is the very highest life of all.

God's joy in our giving

God rejoices in what we give back to him. We are receivers and givers. Similarly, God is not only the Giver, but the Receiver too, and – I say it with reverence – he takes even more pleasure in receiving back from us than in giving to us. Because of our lack of faith we often think that when we give his gifts to us back to him again, they are defiled by our sin. But God says, 'No, they come back to me beautiful and glorified.' The surrender of his dear child, with all his aspirations and thanksgivings, brings the gift back to God with a new value.

Ah, child of God, you do not know how precious the gift which you bring to your Father is in his sight! When a mother gives a piece of cake to her child, how delighted she is when the infant shares it with her! How precious that little piece of cake is to her! And, my friends, the Father's heart of your God longs, longs, longs to have you give everything to him! This is not the demand of a hard master, but

Consecration

the call of a loving Father, who knows that gift you bring to him will bind you closer to himself, and that every surrender you make will open your heart wider to receive more of his spiritual gifts. Friends, a gift to God has infinite value in his sight. It delights him, and it brings unspeakable blessing to you.

Dependence upon God

We have considered the thoughts which our text suggests. Now comes the practical application. What lesson about Christian living can we learn? Simply this: we should live in a state of continual dependence upon God. Become nothing. Begin to understand that you are nothing but an earthen vessel into which God will pour the treasure of his love. Blessed is the man who knows that he is nothing, just a receptacle for God's use. I urge you to come to a state of deep, deep dependence upon God, of child-like trust and expectancy. Count upon our God to do for you everything that you want him to do. Honour God as a God who gives liberally, and believe that he asks nothing from you except what he is first going to give you. Praise him for his willingness to give. Let every sacrifice to him be a thank-offering.

Consecrate your life to him. Come to him and say, 'Lord of all, I belong to you, I am absolutely at your disposal.' Yield yourself to him. You may not necessarily be called to go to the mission field, but you still need to give yourself to God so that you may be consecrated to the work of his Kingdom.

Bow down before him. Give him all of your self — your head to think for his Kingdom, your heart to go out in love for men. However feeble you may be, come and say, 'Lord, here I am, ready to live and die for your Kingdom.'

Some talk and pray about being filled with the Holy Spirit. May they pray more, and believe more. But they should remember that the Spirit came to empower men to be messengers of the gospel. You cannot expect to be filled with the Spirit unless you want to live for Christ's Kingdom. You cannot expect all the love and peace and joy of heaven to come into your life and be your treasures unless you absolutely give them up to the service of God, so that you possess and use them only for him. Only the soul utterly given up to God will receive the fullness of the Holy Spirit.

Dear friends, we must consecrate not only our selves, body and soul, but also everything that we have. Some of you may have children. Perhaps you have only one child, and you dread the very idea of letting him or her go. But remember that God deserves your confidence, your love, your surrender. I plead with you, take your children to Jesus and say to him, 'Anything that pleases you, Lord.' Educate your children for Jesus. God will help you to do it.

Then there is the question of money. I frequently hear appeals for money from missionary societies. I also hear of calculations of what the Christians of England are spending on pleasure, and of how little they are giving to missions. There is something terrible about that. God's children have so much wealth and comfort, and they give away so little!

Consecration

God be praised for every exception to this, but there are many who never give so much that it really costs them something and they feel it. Oh friends, our giving must be in proportion to God's giving! He gives us everything. Let us pray, 'Lord, take it all, every penny I possess. It is all yours.' Let us often say, 'It is all God's.' You may not know how much you should give to God's work. Give it all up, put it all in his hands, and he will teach you if you will wait on him.

So this is the precious message contained in David's words. The first part of it is that our God is willing to give us everything. Then, secondly, we have nothing that we do not receive, and we may receive everything if we are willing to stand before God and take it. Thirdly, whatever we have received from God, we must give back. This brings a second blessing to our souls. Fourthly, whatever God receives back from us gives him infinite joy and happiness, as he sees that his object has been attained. Let us come to God in the spirit of David, with the Spirit of Jesus Christ in us, and pray our prayer of consecration. May the Blessed Spirit give each of us grace to think and to say the right thing, and to do what is pleasing in the Father's sight.

Chapter 2

Surrendering to God's Will

Lord, what wilt thou have me to do?
(Acts 9:6)

People often wonder what the secret was of the amazing power of consecration which we can see in the life of the Apostle Paul. Many different answers have been given to this question. One is that Paul's secret is encapsulated in his words, 'The love of Christ constraineth me' (2 Cor. 5:1), and there is some truth in that view. Other people say the secret is in this profession of faith: 'I can do all things through Christ, which strengtheneth me' (Phil. 4:13), and that belief was indeed one of the key elements of Paul's life. But I want us to look at another verse in Scripture – the very first of Paul's words recorded in the New Testament: 'Lord, what wilt thou have me to do?' I believe that if we want to understand Paul's life as a missionary – if we want

Surrendering to God's Will

to understand his self-sacrifice and devotion — we can do no better than to think about these words in Acts. He gave himself up unreservedly to the living, loving, glorified Christ, so that he might work in his life. He surrendered to the will of Christ. I want to urge both myself and you, with the help of God, to get deeper into the meaning of Paul's example to us.

The question is often and rightly asked, Why is there so much superficial Christianity? I might add, Why is it that so any Christians backslide after an initial experience of conversion and blessing? Why is it that so many appear to be entirely dependent upon their surroundings, so that if they go away to a new district or country, they lose their faith and their power? These questions are of the utmost importance, and the answer to them is of the deepest interest. It is this: these backsliding Christians really have very little personal contact with Christ and God. Their religion does not include an absolute surrender to Christ's will in everything and a waiting upon God for guidance. That is the great trouble with so many Christians. They need to come away from following man and to come into close contact with Jesus Christ.

I have loved missionary work for over fifty years. When I was a schoolboy I had a missionary money box and collecting card, and ever since then have been reading and writing books about missionary work and giving up my time to missions. And yet if you were to ask me, 'Where did you get your initial zeal for missions?' I would have to confess with sadness that it came too much from my Christian upbringing, from dear friends who stirred me up with enthusiasm, from the books which I read. I did not sufficiently realise that it was a matter purely between Christ and myself, that my zeal should have come more directly from the Lord. Had I known that earlier, my consecration to mission work would have been far more entire and used by God.

Christ has a will for every one of us

If Paul had not asked the question, 'Lord, what wilt thou have me to do?' — if he had never manifested such a spirit of surrender — he could never have been used by God as he was. He became an outstanding missionary through believing that God had a plan for him, saying in his heart, 'The will of Christ must from this day rule me; it must have complete mastery over me; I am going to live for it and it alone.' He did not know the full meaning of what he said, he did not know all that God wanted him to do, but he was ready to obey his orders, and Christ accepted that as a surrender to his service for ever.

In Christ, God has a plan for each one of us, just as surely as he had a plan for Paul's life. It covers our whole lives — our every day, every hour, every action. We often ask ourselves questions like these: What must I do for mission work? How much must I give? Do I pray enough? Do I pray in the assurance that the Lord will hear me? Must I give up a child to the mission field (perhaps an only child)? Ought I to take a larger part in stirring up the interest of others? Often we say we don't know the answers to these questions. Why? Because we do not believe that the Lord Jesus has a will concerning us

Surrendering to God's Will

personally. We do not clearly understand that Christ has decided what he wishes us to do and that he will make his will known to us. Christ has to care for millions, but he also cares for every one of us as if we were the only one whom he had in his charge. Christ has a will for my life. That is what really matters. The question of whether he can use me in England or China, India or Africa, is not the chief issue. Am I ready to surrender to his will for my life?

Knowing Christ's will for your life

Of course, in order to surrender to Christ's will, I need to know what it is. People often say, 'It is so difficult to find out what God's will is. I don't know how much I must give. I don't know which mission I should give to, or which mission field I should go to. How can I know the will of God?' I want to say one thing: *Paul believed*. He had just come out of Judaism, and everything was very new to him, but he believed in the Lord. He reasoned in this way: 'He wants me to serve him, so I am sure he will guide me. He will show me what his will is.' And Jesus did show Paul his will — throughout his life. Jesus will make his will known to us too, because that is what we need.

Perhaps this assertion that the Lord will show you his will makes you afraid. You may have known people who have declared that such and such was God's will for their lives, and who have afterwards discovered that they were mistaken. But that is no reason why you should give up trying to know God's will for your life. If someone gave you a false, counterfeit coin today, would you say 'Oh, there are false coins going around — I am not going to accept any more coins at all'? Of course you wouldn't; instead you would take care that no-one else gave you a false coin. So you should indeed beware of counterfeit coinage in this matter of God's guidance, but you should not stop believing that Jesus is willing and able to reveal his will to you.

How blessed a man is when he really knows that he is going to Africa, India, China or wherever in obedience to the will of God and guided by his Spirit! We do so need to believe that the Lord will show us specifically what his will is. There are two types of people in missions and Christian work in general. There are the people who have had their instructions and orders directly *from the Lord*. Paul was not the only one. There are people in our times who come into the same sort of close personal contact with God as he did. But there are also a great many who take things at second-hand. Let us not be among them. Let us take our orders directly from Jesus himself.

The need for surrender

Why is it that so many people complain that God does not show them what his will for them is? I will tell you the answer. Christ reveals his will and his mind only to those who are absolutely surrendered to him. Many people think that they must first ask God to show them what his will is and then do it. But something else is needed first. God wants them to come to him and say, 'Lord, I am thoroughly given up to your will.' He wants them to search their

Surrendering to God's Will

hearts and ask themselves whether they have truly given up the right to have their will or way in anything. I find that this is one of the deepest roots of feebleness in people's Christianity. They do not understand that God wants them to entirely give up their will in everything.

Brother, sister, if you want to have a real mission spirit, if you want to have power for prayer and for work, you must first have the attitude which says, 'Lord, I am truly and entirely given up to your will.' So many people concern themselves with thoughts about their abilities or weaknesses, about the wishes of their families, and settle things without waiting to find out what God's will is. I am not saying that God wants every one of us to go out to Africa or China or India, but I am saying that God wants every one of us to say, 'Lord, I wait absolutely on you to reveal to me your will concerning my work for your Kingdom.'

I will make this clearer by telling a story. The missionary Hudson Taylor was once asked by the mayor of a certain town to come and give an address there. Hudson Taylor agreed, but stipulated that there should be no collection at the meeting. The mayor thought this was very strange, but consented, and then had some posters put up. At the meeting the missionary gave such an impressive message that at the close the mayor stood up and said, 'Our speaker has asked that there should be no collection at this meeting, but I am sure that after such an address many of you will want to give something. So if anything is put into my hand, I will pass it on to Mr Hudson Taylor.' The missionary rose up at once and protested that this was contrary to what had been agreed, and he begged the mayor to say nothing more. As the people left the meeting, various sums of money were put into the mayor's hand, one person giving a five pound note.

Later, at his home, the mayor handed the money over to Hudson Taylor, who still expressed regret. The mayor wanted to know why. The missionary explained that under the impression made by an address people often gave hastily and without much thought. What he had really wanted was that everyone who had attended the meeting should get alone with God afterwards to ask him how much he wanted them to give, and indeed to ask him whether he wanted them to give more than money. There may have been people at the meeting whom God had wanted to go to the mission field, but because of the mayor's appeal they would have given some money, thinking that was an adequate response to the address. And so they would not have prayed over the matter and would not have heard God's call to missionary work. Hudson Taylor wanted people to find out Christ's own, perfect will.

At breakfast the next morning the mayor confessed that when he had gone to his room the night before he had begun to feel that at the meeting he had not really asked the Lord Jesus how much he wanted him to give, and had hastily decided upon the sum of five pounds. That night he had felt that he had to ask himself the question, 'Am I sure that God does not want me to give more?' So instead of five pounds he had decided to give two hundred and fifty — which happened to be the very amount that was needed at the time for a party of missionaries who were going out to China.

Christ is willing to show us his will for our lives, but he will not do this until we come to him personally and say, 'Lord, let your will for me be whatever pleases you; I am wholly given to your glory and your service.'

Dear friends, it is a solemn thing to be in relationship with Christ. I very often feel that people are *playing* with Christ and *playing* at consecration. They may often say, 'I give myself entirely to Jesus,' but, sadly, they do not take time to learn his will. I do not say that this is true of everyone – praise God that there are some who wait for him. But most Christians do not give the Lord time to make known to them what he would have them do.

For the sake of the Kingdom

Too often we tend to apply Paul's question, 'Lord, what wilt thou have me to do?' merely to our own lives. People may ask for God's guidance concerning a particular problem or decision, but they find that they do not get an answer. The reason is this: the Lord Jesus cannot reveal himself fully to us until we are entirely given up to him. Would you spend thousands of pounds on building a house upon a plot of land without knowing for certain that the land truly belonged to you? Similarly, if the Lord Jesus is to spend his love, his trouble, his care and his Holy Spirit on us, do you think he wants to do it before we are utterly surrendered to him? For example, someone might pray, 'Lord, take away my temper,' and not get an answer. This is because they have not said to the Lord, 'Saviour, you know that

I am entirely at your disposal, and that the grace which you bestow upon me will be used for your service and will redound to your glory.'

Why does the Lord want us so keenly? It is so that he may use us *for his Kingdom*. I am sure many of us have to confess — I do so myself with shame — that although we have supported missionary work for a long time, we have looked upon it as a secondary thing, something which can be added on to the Christian life. Many people say, 'I am a Christian, and in addition to that I like to do something for my Lord and his work.' How little we have realised that this must be our attitude: 'Lord, I live from morning to night, from Sunday to Saturday, only as a servant of the King, and the work of your Kingdom and the extension of it is the one thing that I have been redeemed for! I know this truth, and I have given myself up to it. For you and your Kingdom I live, suffer and die.' Such an attitude has the same spirit as Paul's question, 'Lord, what wilt thou have me to do?'

Power to do God's will

The Lord reveals his will to us, and he always gives us the power to perform his will. Someone said to me recently, 'If I give myself so entirely and unconditionally to the Lord, he may ask me to do something very hard. I don't know where he may send me.' So often people do not understand that if they give themselves into the hands of Jesus, they give themselves into the hands of divine, everlasting love. What folly it is to think that the will of God

Surrendering to God's Will 21

may hurt them or may be too heavy for them! A wife may say, 'But suppose God were to take away my husband and children?' Don't listen to the devil when he puts such a question into your mind. Your Father would never do such a thing without giving you abundant grace to cope with it.

Have you ever thought about what the will of God is? It is *the beauty and glory of God* shining out. How does he make his beauty and glory known? *By his will*. When God says, 'Be holy, be righteous, be trustful, be humble,' he makes his will known. Then the perfect beauty of God is shining out in a command.

Have you ever realised that there is no way of climbing up into the heart of God except by his will? God's will is the ladder. You might assume that the going gets more difficult as you climb higher up the ladder, but in fact, the nearer you get to God, the easier and more blessed living becomes. God's power of attraction becomes greater because he is nearer, and he reaches out his hand to draw you up.

The will of God is our blessedness — that is the beauty of it. Every ray of his will, as it shines upon us, makes us more blessed. So do not be afraid to say, 'I want to consecrate myself to the will of Christ. I have been interested in missions in the past, but today I want to make a covenant with Jesus. I consecrate myself absolutely to his will, and I also consecrate my wife and children, my possessions, my property and all that I have. I do not know what his will may be, and I know it may take me some time to find out what it is. But I know Christ has a will for me, and I cast myself into it. A child is not afraid of casting himself into the arms of his mother, so shall I be afraid of casting myself into the arms of Jesus? Lord, I lose myself in your love, in your loving will.'

We must consecrate ourselves to the will of Christ. We know what the essence of that will is: it is his death. He gave his life for perishing souls; we must do the same. The will of Christ is that we should become the servants of the vilest and lowest, as he did. We are to count as loss everything except working so that God may once again have the souls he has made. We are to give ourselves to this task, even though we may feel helpless, feeble and ignorant. We have the assurance that Christ will make us fit for whatever he wants us to do. Paul did not know what lay ahead of him, but he took the right step. Because he had surrendered utterly Christ led him on, and for twenty-five years he was used by God for the blessing of souls.

May God help us to enter into the will of Christ in all things. If we make no conditions and do not stipulate, we may be sure in advance that our heavenly Father will not let us go wrong. Let us trust in the ever-blessed God.

A revelation of Jesus Christ

We now need to ask the question: How can we come to the stage where we are ready to make the sort of full surrender to the will of Christ which we have been thinking about? How can we be so moved and stirred that we are willing to say with the same assurance as Paul had, 'Lord, what wilt thou have me to do?' How did Paul come to have this attitude?

Surrendering to God's Will 23

The answer is simply this: *he had experienced a revelation of Jesus Christ*. The light of God had shone upon him. He had had a vision of heaven, and in it he had seen the face of Jesus, *the King of Glory*. In the light of that revelation he was to live all his remaining years. Someone has expressed Paul's vision in these words:

> *From the glory and the gladness,*
> *From His Holy Place,*
> *From the rapture of His Presence,*
> *From the radiance of His face,*
> *Christ the Son of God has sent me*
> *Through the midnight lands,*
> *Mine the mighty ordination*
> *Of the pierced hands.*

Yes, we too need to get into the Presence of the Glory of the Holy Place, to come with boldness within the veil, where God lets the light of his love in Christ Jesus shine fully upon us. In that Presence we will not have a thought of holding back our consecration, but instead we will say, 'Lord, I am ready – what wilt thou have me to do?'

Do you long for the joy, inspiration and strength to make your consecration? Remember, Christ Jesus belongs to you as much as to Paul. Christ is willing to make himself known to you – he is willing to come near to you, to remain with you, and to say to you, 'I love you with a wonderful love, and I will not rest until I have you in the Father's heart.' Christ comes to you and says, 'My child, my redeemed one, I love you, and I love the perishing heathen, and I died for them. They are the heritage which the

Father has given me. I cannot come down from heaven to die for them again. I cannot go and visit them myself. Will you go?' How will your heart reply to this? Surely it will say, 'My beloved Lord, I will do anything that pleases you. Show me your will, so that I may do it.'

My friends, our mission work must become something very different from what it is at present. You may be praising God for the way in which he has stirred up interest in missions in recent years, and I praise God with you. But we need to take care that this praise does not become self-congratulation. We need to reflect on how the little we are doing compares with what is truly needed and with what Christ wants. I plead with you, consecrate yourself to the crucified Christ for the salvation of the unsaved. Are you ready? Do you believe that the Lord will abundantly equip you to do all that he asks of you?

We need just one thing — personal contact with Jesus, a personal revelation of the Glorified One. What that revelation did for Paul, it will do for us. We only need the light of Christ to shine upon us, and we shall be ready to say, 'I have taken Christ into my heart, and with Christ I have taken the whole world, for Christ belongs to them; now that I belong to him, I belong to them.' Paul prayed, 'Lord, what wilt thou have me to do?' May we now have the grace to pray the same prayer. Our God will hear it and answer it.

Chapter 3

Consecration and Money

> *Jesus . . . beheld how the people cast money into the treasury: and many that were rich cast in much. And there came a certain poor widow, and she threw in two mites, which make a farthing. And he called unto him his disciples, and saith unto them, 'Verily I say unto you, that this poor widow hath cast more in than all they which have cast into the treasury: For all they did cast in of their abundance; but she of her want did cast in all that she had, even all her living.'*
> (Mark 12:41–44)

In all our religion and Bible study it is of the utmost importance that we find out what the mind of Christ is — that we think as he thought and feel as he felt. The words of Christ in Scripture can show us his mind and can offer us guidance and help in all the questions and matters which concern us. In this chapter we are going to think about what the mind of Christ is on the subject of money. We want to know exactly what he thinks about it, so that we can think about it and use it just as he would do.

However, this is not an easy thing. We are so under the influence of the world around us that we very easily fall into the trap of being afraid that we will become utterly unpractical if we try to think and act like Christ. Let us not be afraid. If we truly desire it, he will show us how he wants us to think and what he wants us to do. We only need to be honest in our attitude, saying in our hearts, 'I want Christ to teach me how to possess my money and how to use it.'

How do we think about money in the Church — how do we think about the collection? In our minds we might associate it with some overworked deacon, or with the treasurer of some Christian society. We might even think about Judas, who had charge of the disciples' money. But look at our text for a moment — look at Jesus, sitting there by the treasury, watching the people putting in their gifts. And as he does it, he weighs each gift in the balance of God, and puts a value on it. He still does this in heaven now. There is not a gift, great or small, for any part of God's work which escapes his notice. To each gift he gives a heavenly value. And he is willing to reveal what he thinks of our gifts to our hearts on earth, if they are waiting and prayerful.

Giving money is a part of our Christian life, is watched over by Jesus and must be regulated by his word. Let us try to discover what that word has to teach us on the subject.

Consecration

Giving is a sure test of character

In the world money is the standard of value. It is difficult to express everything that money means. It is often the token of God's blessing on diligent effort. It is the symbol of labour and enterprise and skill. It represents physical and mental work, property, comfort, luxury, influence and power. No wonder the world loves it, seeks it more than anything else and often worships it. No wonder it is the standard of value not only for material things but also for man himself. Very often a man is valued according to his money.

Just as a man is judged by his money in the kingdom of this world, so too he is judged by his money in the Kingdom of Heaven — but by a very different principle. The world asks *what* a man owns; Christ asks *how* he uses what he owns. The world thinks more about the getting of money; Christ thinks about the giving of it. When a man gives, the world wants to know what he gives, while Christ wants to know how he gives. The world looks at the money and its amount; Christ looks at the man and his motive.

We can see all of this in the story of the poor widow. Many rich people were giving a lot of money. But they were giving out of their wealth; they were not making any real sacrifice; their lives would still be as full and comfortable as ever; their gifts cost them nothing and expressed no special love for God or devotion to him. The giving of the rich was part of an easy, traditional religion.

The widow, on the other hand, gave a mere farthing. She was so poor that this was all she had.

She willingly gave everything to God, without reserve.

How different our standard is from Christ's! We ask how much a man gives; Christ asks how much he keeps. We look at the gift; Christ asks whether the gift was a sacrifice. The widow sacrificed everything she had. Her gift won Christ's heart and approval, because it was given in the spirit of his own self-sacrifice. He had been rich and had become poor for our sakes.

But if our Lord wanted us to give as she did, why didn't he leave a clear command about it? How gladly we would then do it! Ah, but there you have it! We want a command to make us do it. But that would pander to the spirit of the world. We would then give supreme importance to what we were giving, to the fact that we were giving everything. And that is just what Christ does not wish and will not have. Instead he wants the generous love which gives all without being told to. He wants every gift to be warm and bright with love, a true free-will offering.

If you want the Master's approval as the poor widow had it, remember one thing: you must put everything at his feet and at his disposal. And that must be the spontaneous expression of a love which cannot help giving, just because it loves. What a test of character our giving is! Lord Jesus, give us the grace to love you deeply, so that we may know how to give to you.

Giving is a great means of grace

Christ called his disciples to him so that he could teach them about the giving which he had seen at

Consecration

the treasury. That teaching guides us just as it guided them. If we listen to Christ with a real desire to learn, our giving will have a great influence upon our spiritual growth.

Money is the principal means which the world has of gratifying its desires − of satisfying 'the lust of the flesh the lust of the eye and the pride of life' (1 John 2:16). Christ has said about his people, 'They are not f the world, as I am not of the world' (John 17:16). They are to show by the way in which they use their money that they live by unworldly principles, that the Spirit of heaven teaches them how to use their wealth. And what does that Spirit teach us? To use our money for spiritual purposes, for what will last for eternity, for what is pleasing to God.

'They that are Christ's have crucified the flesh and its lusts' (Gal. 5:24). One of the ways of manifesting and maintaining that crucifixion of the flesh is to never use money to gratify it. And the way to conquer every temptation to do so is to have the heart filled with large thoughts of the spiritual power of money. Do you want to keep the flesh crucified? Refuse to spend a penny on its gratification. Just as surely as money spent on self nourishes and strengthens self, so money sacrificed to God helps the soul to be victorious over the world and the flesh.

Our whole life of faith may be strengthened by the way in which we deal with money. Many people have to be continually occupied with making money in their daily work. There is a danger that their hearts may be dragged down and bound to earth through their dealings with what is the very life of the world. Faith can ensure a continual victory over this temptation. Every thought of the danger of money, every effort to resist it, every loving gift to God, helps our life of faith. Through faith we look at things from God's perspective and judge them by heavenly standards. And so the money which passes through our hands and which we devote to God becomes a daily education in faith and heavenly-mindedness.

Our giving of money will also strengthen our life of love. Every grace needs to be exercised if it is to grow; this is true above all of love. We need to understand that as we are called upon to give to others, we are made to consider their needs carefully and sympathetically, and so it is that our money can develop and strengthen our love. Every call for money which we hear and every response we make can be an occasion for the stirring of a new depth of love in us, and an opportunity for us to make a fuller surrender to love's blessed claims.

Do believe this. The giving of your money can be one of the most powerful means for you to receive God's grace. By it you can prove the earnestness of your heart's desire to walk before God in self-denial, faith and love. Through the renewal of your surrender of your whole life to God, you will know a continuous fellowship with him.

Giving is a wonderful power for God

What a wonderful religion Christianity is. It takes money — the very embodiment of the power of this world, the very essence of the world's self-interest, covetousness and pride — and changes it into an instrument for the service and glory of God.

Think of the poor. What help and happiness is brought to tens of thousands of helpless ones by the timely gift of a little money from the hand of love. God has allowed the difference between rich and poor for this very purpose — that just as by the interchange of buying and selling mutual dependence is maintained among men, so in the giving and receiving of charity there should be abundant scope for the blessing of doing and receiving good. Jesus said, 'It is more blessed to give than to receive' (Acts 20:35). What a God-like privilege it is to have the power of relieving the needy and making the hearts of the poor glad through the giving of money! How blessed we Christians are in that the money we give away is a source of greater pleasure to us than that which we spend on ourselves! The latter is mostly spent on what is temporal and carnal; that which is spent on the work of love has eternal value, and brings happiness to ourselves and to others too.

Think of the Church and its work, of missions at home and abroad, of the thousand different agencies which exist for the purpose of winning men from sin to God and holiness. Is it really true that the coin of this world, by being cast into God's treasury in the right spirit, can receive the stamp of the mint of heaven, and can be accepted in exchange for heavenly blessings? It is true. The gifts which we give in faith and love do not merely go into the Church's treasury, but also go into God's own treasury, and are paid out again in the form of heavenly goods. Those goods are not to be judged according to the earthly standard of value, where the question is always 'How much?' but according to the standard of heaven, where men's judgements of much and little, great and small, are completely unknown.

Christ immortalised a widow's farthing. It shines through the ages with the glory of heavenly value, brighter because of Christ's approval than the brightest gold. By the lesson it has taught it has been a blessing to countless people. It teaches me that my farthing, if it is my everything, if it is honestly given as all that I ought to give the Lord at the present time, has his approval, his stamp, his eternal blessing.

If we would only take more time to meditate on this and allow the Holy Spirit to show us the Lord Jesus in charge of the Heavenly Mint, stamping every true gift and then using it for the Kingdom, surely our money would begin to shine with a new lustre. And we would begin to say, 'The less I can spend on myself, and the more on my Lord, the richer I am.' And we shall see that the person who truly gives all he can is the richest of all, just as the widow was richer through her gift than the many rich people.

Giving is a continual help on the ladder to heaven

There are many who would pay a great deal for heaven if it could be bought. But we can no more purchase heaven with money than we can with works. And yet money can indeed wonderfully help us along on the path of holiness and heaven. Through our giving, heavenly-mindedness, love for Christ and for men, and devotion to God's work are cultivated and proved in us. Money given in the

Consecration

spirit of self-sacrifice, of love for and faith in the One who has paid the price for us brings a rich and eternal reward. Giving day by day as God enables and asks us will help bring heaven nearer to us, and will bring us nearer to heaven. Our giving can prepare us for heaven.

The Christ who sat by the treasury is your Christ. He watches your gifts. He accepts the things which you give in a spirit of wholehearted devotion and love. He teaches his disciples to judge as he judges. He will teach you how to give and how much to give; he will show you how to give lovingly and truthfully.

Money is the cause of so much temptation, sin, sorrow and eternal loss. We need to learn from Jesus, the Lord of the Heavenly Treasury, that when it is received and distributed at his feet, money becomes one of the most powerful means for the channelling of God's grace into our lives and the lives of others. Lord, give all of us in your Church the spirit of the poor widow who gave everything to you!

Chapter 4

Perfect in Christ

God was pleased to make known what is the riches of the glory of this mystery . . . which is Christ in you, the hope of glory: Whom we proclaim, admonishing every man and teaching every man in all wisdom, that we may present every man perfect in Christ; Whereunto I labour also, striving according to his working, which worketh in me mightily.

(Colossians 1:27–2)

There are three aspects to the truth that we are perfect in Christ. First, there is *our perfection in Christ as it is prepared for us in him, our Head.* Christ, the second Adam, has given a new nature to all the members of his body. This nature is his own life, which was perfected through suffering and

Perfect in Christ 35

obedience. Having been perfected himself, he has thereby also perfected those who are sanctified through him. His perfection, his perfect life, is ours — and not merely in a legal sense or by imputation, but also as a reality which we can experience through our living union with him. Paul says elsewhere in this epistle, 'Ye are complete, made full in him.' We are fulfilled in Christ: circumcised in him, buried with him, raised with him, made alive with him.

Secondly, there is our perfection in Christ *as imparted to us by the Holy Spirit as he unites us with Jesus in conversion*. The life which is implanted in us at the new birth, in the midst of a person of sin and flesh, is a perfect life. As the seed contains in itself the whole of the life of the tree, so the seed of God within us contains the perfect life of Christ, with its power to grow, fill our lives and yield perfect fruit.

Thirdly, there is our perfection in Christ as *appropriated by us through the obedience of faith and so made manifest in our life and conduct*. As our faith grasps and feeds upon the truth of the two former aspects, and yields itself to God so that the perfect life may master and pervade the whole of our daily life in its ordinary activities, perfection in Christ will become a practical reality and experience at every moment. All that the word of God has taught us about the perfect heart and the perfect life, about being perfect like the Father and perfect like the Master, is revealed to us with new meaning. The living Christ is our perfection; he himself lives every day and every hour in order to impart it to us. The measureless love of Jesus, and the power of the endless life in which he works, become the measure of our expectation. Through the life which we now live, with its daily duties, its intercourse with people and money, its cares and temptations, we are to prove that perfection in Christ is no mere ideal, but in the power of Almighty God is simple and literal truth.

In our text Paul speaks of admonishing and teaching every man, in all wisdom, so that he may present him perfect in Christ Jesus. He is here talking about the last of these three aspects of perfection in Christ — that perfection as it is seen in the daily life of the believer. In theory, the Christians to whom he was writing were perfect in Christ; in practice they had yet to become perfect. The aim of his gospel ministry among them was to bring each one of them to perfection in Christ, to teach them how they could put on the Lord Jesus and have his life covering them and indwelling them.

What a task! As the minister considers the state of his church, it might seem a hopeless one. And yet if he does his work as Paul did it, he has cause for infinite hope. He said, 'I labour, striving according to his working, which worketh in me mightily.' The aim of the ministry is high, but the power to achieve it is divine. May each minister, with all his heart, make Paul's goal his own, and may he, like Paul, count upon God to enable him to realise that goal.

Chapter 5

Perfect in All the Will of God

Epaphras, who is one of you, a servant of Christ Jesus, saluteth you, always striving for you in his prayers, that ye may stand perfect and fully assured in all the will of God.
(Colossians 4:12)

In this epistle, as in some others, we are shown the life of the believer as he lives it in heaven in Christ, and also as he lives it here on earth with men. The teaching of Scripture is intensely spiritual and supernatural, but at the same time it is truly human and practical. Earlier in the epistle (1:27–29) Paul says his goal is to make the believers 'perfect in Christ'. This expresses the former of these two aspects of scriptural teaching; the latter is expressed by the verse quoted above, in which we read that Epaphras, another minister of the gospel, prays that the believers might be perfect 'in all the will of God'.

'Perfect in Christ.' This thought is so unearthly and divine that its full meaning eludes our grasp. It makes us think of our life in Christ and heaven. 'Perfect in all the will of God.' This thought bring us down to earth and daily life; it reminds us that we must place everything under God's rule, and calls us to live in his will, obeying him in our every action and attitude.

The perfection of the creature is simply this: to will the will of the Creator. Nature has its beauty and glory in being the expression of the divine will. The angels fulfil their purpose by doing God's will in heaven. The Son of God was perfected through learning obedience, through giving himself up to the will of God. The redemption which he has achieved has only one purpose − to bring man into the will of God, which is the only place of true rest and blessedness.

The prayer of Epaphras shows how truly he has entered into the Spirit of his Master. He prays that the believers may stand in the will of God − more than that, in *all* the will of God. He wanted there to be not a single aspect of their lives which was not in God's will. Note also that they were to be *perfect* in all the will of God − they were to walk in a perfect way at each moment with a perfect heart. To his mind this was the very best prayer which he could pray for them.

Paul prays that the Colossians might be 'filled with the knowledge of [God's] will in all spiritual wisdom and understanding' (1:9). So both he and Epaphras are of one mind that young converts need to be reminded that their knowledge of God's will

Perfect in All the Will of God

is very defective, that they need to pray for divine teaching in order to know that will, and that their one aim should be to stand perfect in all that will.

All seekers after perfection should note that lesson well. While rightly rejoicing in a consecration sealed by the Holy Spirit and conscious that his devotion to God is whole-hearted, a believer may be tempted to forget that there may be many things about which he does not yet know God's will. There may be grave defects in his character and a serious failure to fulfil the law of perfect love in his behaviour; others may be able to perceive these things in him while he is as yet unaware of them. Being sure that we are living up to the full light of what we know to be right is a great blessing, and is one of the traits of the perfect heart. But it must always be accompanied by an awareness of how much there may be which has not yet been revealed to us.

This sense of ignorance of much of God's will, this conviction that there is still much in us that needs to be changed and sanctified and perfected, will make us very humble and tender, very watchful and hopeful in prayer. Far from interfering with our assurance that we serve God with a perfect heart, this cautiousness will give it new strength, while cultivating humility, which is the greatest beauty of perfection. Without this humbleness our consciousness of our uprightness becomes superficial and dangerous, and the doctrine of perfection becomes a stumblingblock and a snare.

To be 'perfect in all the will of God' — may this be our unceasing aim and prayer. May we be deeply conscious of how much has yet to be revealed to us, may we be strengthened by the awareness that we have given ourselves to serve God with a perfect heart, may we be joyfully content with nothing less than standing perfect in all the will of God, and may we rejoice in the knowledge of what God will do for those who are perfect in Christ Jesus. May our faith claim the full blessing. God will reveal to us that being perfect in Christ Jesus and being perfect in all the will of God are one and the same in his mind, and that they may be so in our experience.

Chapter 6

Not Perfected, Yet Perfect

> *Not that I have already obtained, or am already made perfect: but I press on . . . one thing I do . . . I press on toward the goal . . . Let us therefore, as many as be perfect, be thus minded.*
> (Philippians 3:12–15)

There are degrees of perfection. There is perfect, more perfect and most perfect. There is being perfect, and waiting to be perfected. So it was with our Lord Jesus. In Hebrews we read three times that he was perfected or made perfect. Of course, there was never the faintest shadow of sinful imperfection in him. At each moment of his life he was perfect, he was just what he ought to be. And yet he needed to be perfected through suffering and the obedience which he learned from it. As he conquered temptation and maintained his allegiance to God, and with agonised crying and tears gave up his will to God's will, his human nature was perfected, and he became a High Priest, 'a Son, perfected for evermore' (Heb. 7:28). During his life on earth Jesus was perfect, and not yet perfected.

The perfected disciple will be like his Master (Luke 6:4). What is true of Jesus is true, in our measure, of us too. Paul wrote to the Corinthians about speaking wisdom among the perfect, a wisdom which carnal Christians could not understand. Here in our text he classes himself with the perfect, and includes his readers in the same category. He sees no difficulty in speaking of himself and others as perfect, or in speaking of the perfect as needing to be further and more fully perfected.

So what is this perfection which has yet to be perfected? And who are these perfect people? The man who has chosen the highest perfection, and who has given his whole heart and life to attain it, is counted a perfect man by God. 'The kingdom of heaven is like unto a grain of mustard seed' (Matt. 13:31). Where God sees in the heart the single purpose of being all that God wills, he sees the divine seed of all perfection. And as he counts faith as righteousness, so he counts that whole-hearted purpose as perfection. The man with a perfect heart is accepted by God as a perfect man, despite all the imperfections of his actual life. So Paul could look upon the Philippian church and talk about those who were 'perfect'.

He described two classes of Christians among the Corinthian believers. The large majority were carnal and content to live in conflict with one another. The

Not Perfected, Yet Perfect

minority were spiritual and perfect. I am afraid that in the Church of our own day the great majority of believers have no conception of their calling to be perfect. They have not the slightest idea that it is their duty not only to be spiritual, but to be as thoroughly spiritual, as full of grace and holiness, as it is possible for God to make them. Even in those who have a certain degree of serious commitment to the pursuit of holiness, there is such a lack of faith in the earnestness of God's desire to make them perfect and in the sufficiency of his grace to bring it about, that they make little progress. In no real sense do they understand or accept Paul's invitation: 'Let us therefore, as many as be perfect, be thus minded.'

But thank God, this is not the case with all Christians. There is an ever-increasing number who cannot forget that Christ means what he says when he gives the command, 'Be perfect' (Matt. 5:48). They see themselves as under the most binding obligation to obey the command. The words, 'Be perfect' are to them a revelation of what Christ has come to give to them and do in them; they are a promise of the blessing to which his teaching and leading will bring them. They have joined the group of likeminded ones whom Paul associated with himself; they seek God with their whole heart; they serve him with perfect heart; their one aim in life is to be made perfect, even as the Master is perfect.

The mark of the perfect, as we see in the case of Paul, is the passionate desire to be made perfect. This looks like a paradox. And yet what we see in the life of our Master proves the truth of it. A consciousness of being perfect is in entire harmony with a readiness to sacrifice life itself for the sake of being made perfect. It was so with Christ, and with Paul. It will be so with us as we open our hearts fully and give God's words room and time to do their work. It is often thought that the more imperfect someone is, the more he will feel his need of perfection. But all experience, in every department of life, teaches us that it is those who are nearest to perfection who are the most aware of their need to still be perfected, and who are the most ready to make any sacrifice to attain to it. To count everything as loss compared with perfection is the surest proof that perfection in principle has claimed possession of the heart. The more honestly and earnestly the believer seeks God with a perfect heart, the more ready will he be to say with Paul, 'not that I have already obtained, or am already perfected.'

And in what respect is it that Paul longs to be made perfect? Read the wonderful passage in which our text occurs with care and without preconceived ideas, and I think you will see that he gives no indication *here* that it is sin or sinful imperfection from which he is seeking to be perfectly free. Whatever his writings say elsewhere, that thought is not in his mind here. The perfected disciple is perfect like his Master. What Paul is talking about here is his life and his life's work. He feels that they will not be perfected until he has reached the goal and obtained the prize. He is pressing on towards this.

Someone running in a race may, in the middle of it, have so far done everything perfectly. Everyone may agree that he has run perfectly so far. And yet the race is not finished, and so his part in it is not yet perfected. So Paul is not talking about failure or shortcoming but about what is as yet unfinished and waiting for its full end. He uses expressions which tell us that what he has so far experienced of Christ is just a part of the full reality. He knows Christ, he has gained Christ, he is found in him, he has in a wonderful way taken hold of that blessing for which Christ has taken hold of him. And yet he now speaks of all these things as that which he is still striving after with all his might: 'If by any means I may attain unto the resurrection from the dead . . . I press on toward the goal unto the prize' (11, 14). This is what he means when he says, 'Not that I am already . . . made perfect' (12).

Paul has known Christ for many years, but he knows that in Christ there are riches and treasures greater than he has yet known, and nothing can satisfy him but the full and final and eternal possession of what the resurrection will bring him. For this he considers all other things as loss; for this he forgets what has happened in the past; for this he presses on towards the goal, towards the prize.

Christian, learn here the price of perfection, as well as the mark of the perfect ones. The Master gave his life to be made perfect for ever. Paul did the same. It is a very serious thing to pursue perfection. The pearl of great price is dear: everything must be considered as loss compared to it.

I urge you to enrol in the class of the perfect. Ask the Master to put your name down on the list and give you the blessed assurance which the Spirit gives to a perfect heart. If, like Paul, you claim to be perfect, single-minded and whole-hearted in your surrender to God, live the life of the perfect, with

All things loss for Jesus as your watchword and your strength, your one desire being to possess him wholly, to be possessed by him, to be made perfect, just as he was.

Chapter 7

The Divine Standard

> *Be ye therefore perfect, even as your Father which is in heaven is perfect.*
> (Matthew 5:48)

Perfect before God, perfect with God, perfect towards God — these are expressions which we find in the Old Testament. They all refer to a relationship, to the choice or purpose of the heart devoted to God, to the whole-hearted desire to trust and obey him. The words from the New Testament quoted above, however, lift us up to a very different level, and open up to us what Christ has done for us. Now we can be not only perfect towards God, but also *perfect like God*. This verse reveals the wonderful prospect which is held out to us. It shows us the infinite fullness of meaning which the word 'perfect' has in God's mind. It gives us the only standard we are to aim at and judge by. It casts down all hopes of perfection as a human attainment, and yet awakens hope in the God who has the power and the will to make us like himself.

A young child may be the perfect image of his father. There is a great difference in age, stature and power between them, and yet the resemblance may be so striking that everyone notices it. And so a child of God, although infinitely less than the Father, may yet bear his image and likeness so markedly that in his creaturely life he is as perfect as the Father is. This is possible. It is what Jesus commands. It is what each one of us should aim at. Being perfect as our Father in heaven is perfect must become one of the first articles of our creed, one of the guiding lights of our Christian life.

What this perfection of the Father consists of is apparent from the passage in which our text occurs: 'Love your enemies . . . that ye may be children of your Father which is in heaven . . . Be ye therefore perfect, even as your Father which is in heaven is perfect' (verses 4, 45, 8). Alternatively, in Luke's Gospel we have the wording, 'Be ye therefore merciful, as your Father also is merciful' (6:36). God's perfection is his love, his will to share his own blessedness with all around him. His compassion and mercy are the glory of his being. He created us in his image and after his likeness, in order that we should find our glory in a life of love and mercy and blessing. We are to be perfect in love, even as our Father is perfect.

Immediately we ask the question, 'But is it possible? And if so, how?' It is certainly not possible through man's efforts. But Christ's command itself contains the answer to our question: 'Be perfect as

The Divine Standard 49

your Father is perfect.' It is because the little child has received his life from his father, and because his father watches over his training and development, that there can be such a striking and ever-increasing resemblance between them. It is because the sons of God are partakers of the divine nature and have God's life, Spirit and love within them that Christ's command is reasonable, and our obedience is possible, in ever-increasing measure. The perfection is our Father's. We have its seed within us; he delights in making it increase. The words which first appear to cast us down in utter helplessness now become our hope and strength: 'Be perfect, as *your Father* is perfect.' Claim your heritage; give yourself up wholly to be a child of God; yield yourself to the Father, so that he may do in you all that he is able to do.

We also need to remember who it is who gives this message from the Father to us. It is the Son, who was himself perfected by the Father through suffering, who learned obedience and was made perfect, and who has perfected us for ever. The message, 'Be perfect,' comes to us from the Son as a promise inspiring infinite hope. What he asks, he gives; what he speaks, he does.

To 'present every man perfect in Christ' (Col. 1:28) is the one aim of Christ and his gospel. Let us accept the command from him; in yielding ourselves to obey it, let us yield ourselves to him. We should let our hope and expectation be in Christ, in whom we have been perfected. Through faith in Christ we receive the Holy Spirit, by whom the love of God fills our hearts. Through faith in Christ that love becomes in us a fountain of love springing up ceaselessly. In our union with Christ the love of God is perfected in us, and we are perfected in love. So we should not be afraid to obey the command, 'Be perfect, as your Father is perfect.'

Chapter 8

Jesus, the Model of Perfection

> *Be ye therefore merciful, as your Father also is merciful . . . The disciple is not above his master: but every one that is [perfected] shall be as his master.*
>
> (Luke 6:36, 40)

Matthew and Luke record this section of Jesus' Sermon on the Mount in slightly different words. We should notice that like Matthew, Luke uses the word 'perfect', but with reference to the Son, as the Master of his disciples, rather than to the Father. This change is most instructive, since it leads us to consider Jesus, in his life as a man, as our model. It might be said that our circumstances and powers are so different from those of God that it is impossible to apply the standard of his infinite perfection in our little world. But here comes the

Son, in the likeness of sinful humanity, tempted in every way as we are, offering himself as our Master and Leader. He lives with us so that we may live with him; he lives in us so that we may live like him.

So the divine standard has been embodied and made visible and brought within our reach by a human model. In growing into the likeness of Christ, who is the image of the Father, we shall come to bear the likeness of the Father too. Becoming like Christ, we shall become perfect, as our Father is. 'The disciple is not above his Master: but every one that is perfect shall be as his master.'

One aspect of the disciple's resemblance to his Master is outward humiliation: like the Master, he will be despised and persecuted (Matt. 1:24-25; John 15:20). Another aspect is inward humility, a willingness to be a servant (Luke 22:27; John 13:16). The perfected disciple knows of nothing higher than being like his Master both in his outward behaviour and his inner attitude.

To take Jesus as Master, with the distinct desire and aim of living and acting like him — this is true Christianity. This is something far more than accepting him as a Saviour and Helper, far more even than acknowledging him as Lord and Master. Only this is full discipleship: to long to be as much like the Master as possible in everything, to count his life as the true expression of all that is perfect, and to aim at nothing less than being perfect, as he was.

'Every one that is perfected shall be as his master.' The words suggest to us very distinctly that there is more than one stage in discipleship. In the Old Testament we can read about people who served the

Jesus, the Model of Perfection   53

Lord with a perfect heart, and about others who did not (l Kings 11:4; 15:3; 2 Chron. 25:2). In the same way, there are great differences between disciples now. There are some who have never realised that they can aim at the perfect likeness of the Master: they only look to Christ as a Saviour. And there are some whose hearts indeed long for full conformity to their Lord, but who have never understood that there is such a thing as 'a perfect heart' and a life 'perfected in love', even though they have read these words. But there are also those who have understood and accepted these words in their divine meaning and truth and who can say with Hezekiah, 'I have walked before thee with a perfect heart' (2 Kings 20:3), and with John, 'as he is, even so are we in this world' (1 John 4:19). As we go on in our study of what Scripture says about perfection, let us hold on to the principle which we have learned here. We are to aspire to likeness to Jesus, to his humiliation and humility. Like him, we are to choose the nature of a servant, and the spirit which does not exercise lordship and does not seek to be ministered to, but rather holds itself ready to minister to others and to give its life for them. This is the secret of true perfection. With the perfect love of God as our standard, with that love revealed in Christ's humanity and humility, with Christ as our model and our guide, with the Holy Spirit to strengthen us with might so that Jesus may live in us, we shall learn to know what it is to be perfect.

Chapter 9

May the God of Peace Perfect You

Now the God of peace, who brought again from the dead the great shepherd of the sheep with the blood of the eternal covenant, even our Lord Jesus, make you perfect in every good thing to do his will, working in us that which is well-pleasing in his sight, through Jesus Christ; to whom be the glory for ever and ever. Amen.
(Hebrews 13:20–21)

These two verses contain a summary of the whole Epistle to the Hebrews in the form of a prayer. In verse 20 we have the essence of what was taught in the first, doctrinal half of the epistle — that is, that God has redeemed us through Jesus Christ. Verse 21 sums up the second, practical half of the epistle,

May the God of Peace Perfect You   55

in which the outcome and fruit of that redemption — the life in the fullness of faith and hope and of love and good works — was set before us. In this prayer, which is a revelation and a promise of what the God of redemption will do for us, we see how his one aim and desire is *to make us perfect*.

We need a large faith to claim this promise. In order that our faith may be full and strong, we are reminded in these verses of what God is and what he has done — this is the assurance of what he will be to us and do for us. Let us look to him as the God of peace, who has made peace by completely putting away sin; who now proclaims peace; who gives perfect peace. Let us look to Jesus Christ, the Great Shepherd of the sheep, our High Priest and King, who loves to care for us and look after us. The power which raised Jesus from the dead is also the power which works in us. So let us think about his resurrection, so that our faith and hope will be in God. Let us remember the blood of the eternal covenant, in the power of which Jesus was raised and entered heaven — that blood is God's pledge that the covenant, with its promises, will be fulfilled in our hearts.

Yes, let us look upon and worship and adore this God of peace, who has done it all, who has raised Christ through the blood of the covenant, so that we might know and trust him. And let us believe the message which tells us that this God of peace will perfect us in every good thing. The God who perfected Christ will perfect us too. The God who has worked out such a perfect salvation for us will perfect it in us. The more we gaze upon the One who has done such wonderful things for us, the more we will trust him to do the wonderful thing which he promises to do in us — to perfect us in every good thing. What God did in Christ is the measure of what he will do to make us perfect. The same Omnipotence which worked in Christ to perfect him waits for our faith to trust its working in us day by day as we do God's will. And on our part, our surrender in order to be made perfect will be the measure of our capacity to apprehend what God has done in Christ.

Now let us think about what this perfection is. It is truly divine, as divine as the work of redemption: it is *the God of peace himself*, who raised Christ from the dead, who perfects us. It is intensely practical: we are to do his will in every *good thing*. It is universal, and nothing is excluded from its effect: we are to be perfect in *every* good thing. It is truly human and personal: God perfects us, so that *we do his will*. It is inward: God works *in us* what is pleasing in his sight. And it is most blessed, giving us the assurance that our life pleases him, because it is his own work: he works in us *what is pleasing in his sight*.

May God perfect you to do his will: this is the conclusion of the whole matter. To do his will: this is the blessedness of the angels in heaven. For this the Son became man; by this he was perfected; in this we are sanctified. It is in order that we may do his will that God perfects us and brings about within us what is pleasing in his sight.

Believer, let God's aim be yours. Say to God that you do desire this more than anything else. Give yourself to this at once, entirely, absolutely, and say with the Son, 'I come to do your will, O my God.'

May the God of Peace Perfect You 57

This will give you an insight into the meaning and the need and the preciousness of the promise that God will perfect you to do his will. This will fix your heart upon God in the wonderful light of the truth that he who perfected Christ is perfecting you too. This will give you confidence, in the fullness of faith, to claim this God as your God, the God who perfects you in every good thing.

Yes, the Christian who dares say to God that he yields himself to do his will in everything, and abides by his vow despite all the humiliation caused by his sense of emptiness and impotence, will be given the strength to rise and to appropriate and experience in full measure what God has offered in his precious word — that is, the promise that the God of peace will perfect him 'in every good thing to do his will', bringing about in him that which is pleasing in his sight, through Jesus Christ. And that Christian will sing this song of adoring love with new understanding and in the fullness of joy: 'To him be glory for ever and ever! Amen!'

Chapter 10

Perfected by God Himself

And the God of all grace, who called you unto his eternal glory in Christ, after that ye have suffered a little while, shall himself perfect, stablish, strengthen you. To him be the dominion for ever and ever. Amen.
(1 Peter 5:10–11)

Through suffering to glory: this is the keynote of the First Epistle of Peter. The word 'suffer' occurs sixteen times, the word 'glory' fourteen times. Peter sums up all that he has taught his readers in the epistle with the words quoted above. In no other epistle in the New Testament are the two aspects of Christ's death — that he suffered for us, and that we are to suffer with him and like him — so clearly and closely linked together. Fellowship with Christ and likeness to Christ, manifested in suffering, is

Perfected by God Himself

the point of view from which Peter wants us to look upon life as the path to glory.

To be a partaker of the sufferings and the glory of Christ is the Christian's privilege. It was through suffering that God made the Leader of our salvation perfect, so that he could lead many sons to glory. In the verses which we have quoted Peter is talking about our following our Leader in suffering so that we can be made ready for his glory. 'The God of all grace' — the God who is so infinitely gracious, who has grace for every need — 'who called you unto his eternal glory, after that ye have suffered a little while, *shall himself perfect you.*'

Perfection is in God alone, and all perfection comes from him. Consider the wonderful perfection of the sun — the laws it obeys, the blessings it radiates. All of it is by the will of the Creator. Its perfection comes from God. And so, through the whole of nature, from the tiniest insect that floats in the sunbeam to the humblest little flower that basks in its light, everything owes its beauty to God alone. All his works praise him. All his works are perfect.

So we see in Creation the open secret of Christian perfection. It is God who must perfect us. What is revealed to us in nature is the pledge of what is secured for us in grace. 'For it became him, for whom are all things, and through whom are all things, in bringing many sons unto glory, to make the author [or leader] of their salvation perfect through sufferings' (Heb. 2:10). It is fitting that God should show that he is the God who brings about perfection amidst the weakness and suffering of a human life. This is the very essence of salvation: to be perfected by God; to yield oneself to God, for whom and through whom all things exist, in order to be perfected by him.

God has planted the desire for perfection deep in the heart of man. It is this desire which stirs the spirit of the artist, the poet, the craftsman, the inventor, the scientist. In these fields it is the nearest possible approach to perfection which elicits admiration and enthusiasm. In the spiritual realm, is it the case that perfection can only be known in grace and by imputation? Certainly not, if God's word is true. 'God shall himself perfect you,' it says, and he will also 'stablish [and] strengthen you'. The perfecting by God which it speaks of refers to our actual experience, to our present daily lives.

O soul, learn to know this perfecting God, and claim him as yours! Worship and adore him until you are filled with the assurance that your God is perfecting you. Think of yourself as clay in the hands of the Great Artist, who is spending all his time and thought and love on making you perfect. Yield yourself in voluntary, loving obedience to his will and his Spirit. Let every bud or flower you come across be a messenger whispering to you, 'Just let your God work in you; just wait upon God; God himself will perfect you.'

Believer, do you long to be perfected? Oh, claim it, claim it now — or rather, claim the God who perfects! Just as Peter and the writer of Hebrews gather up all their varied teaching into the one central promise that 'God himself will perfect you,' so in the life of the believer there may come a moment when he gathers up all his desires and efforts, all his knowledge of God's truth and all his faith in

Perfected by God Himself

God's promises, concentrates them in one simple act of surrender and trust and, yielding himself completely to do his will, dares to claim God as the God who perfects him. And his life becomes one doxology of adoring love: 'To him be the dominion for ever and ever. Amen.'

Chapter 11

Keeping Christ's Word

Whoso keepeth his word, in him verily hath the love of God been perfected.
(1 John 2:5)

The writer Tauler says of the Apostle John:

> In three ways, dear children, did the beloved Lord attract to Himself the heart of John.
> First, did the Lord Jesus call him out of the world to make him an apostle.
> Next, did He grant to him to rest upon His loving breast.
> Thirdly, and this was the greatest and most perfect nearness, when on the holy day of Pentecost, He gave to him the Holy Ghost, and opened to him the door through which he should pass into the heavenly places.
> Thus, children, does the Lord first call you from

the world, and make you to be the messengers of God. And next, He draws you close to Himself, that you may learn to know His holy gentleness and loveliness, and His deep and burning love, and His perfect unshrinking obedience.

And yet this is not all. Many have been drawn thus, and are satisfied to go no farther. And yet they are far from the perfect nearness which the heart of Jesus desires.

St John lay at one moment on the breast of the Lord Jesus, and then he forsook Him and fled.

If you have been brought so far as to rest on the breast of Christ, it is well. But yet there was to John a nearness still to come, one moment of which would be worth a hundred years of all that had gone before. The Holy Ghost was given to him — the door was opened.

There is a nearness in which we lose ourselves, and God is all in all. This may come to us in one swift moment, or we may wait for it with longing hearts, and learn to know it at last. It was of this St Paul spoke when he said that the thing which the heart hath not conceived, God hath now revealed to us by the Holy Spirit. The soul is drawn within the inner chamber, and there are the wonders and the riches revealed.

Three Friends of God by Mrs Bevan

In order to understand a writer it is often necessary to know his character and history. When John wrote this epistle he had for fifty years been living in that nearness to Jesus which Tauler describes. He had been living in the inner chamber, within the veil. While Jesus was on earth John had been his close friend, able to understand his highest spiritual teaching, one for whom he felt special love. At the time of writing he had had fifty years of knowing the Son in the glory of the Father, of experiencing the power of the Holy Spirit to make the eternal life — the heavenly life of Jesus in fellowship with the Father — an everyday reality. He describes it as a life of perfect love. Christians who are not living on that level can speak of such a life only as an unattainable ideal. And yet, from what we know of what John was and what he knew of his Lord, and what a church under his teaching would be like, we must conclude that his words are simply descriptive of the Christians whom he knew. They were people to whom he could write, 'Beloved, if our hearts condemn us not, we have boldness toward God . . . because we keep his commandments, and do the things that are pleasing in his sight'; 'Whoso keepeth his word, in him verily hath the love of God been perfected' (3:21–22; 2:5).

John was the disciple whom Jesus loved, so the words which Jesus spoke about the love of God had a special attraction for him; the love with which Jesus loved him exercised a mighty influence in his life. After Pentecost the Holy Spirit, coming from the heart of the glorified Jesus, intensified and spiritualised it all, and so John became the Apostle of Love who, gazing into the very depths of the Divine Glory and Being, discovered there that God is love.

This word 'love' was the sum of his theology, and he linked it with a word which he had found in the Old Testament and in the writings of his brother apostles — the word 'perfection'. He tells us that the highest perfection of Christian character and the highest attainment of the Christian life is this — that a man should have *God's love perfected in him*.

John recorded these words of Jesus about being perfected in love: 'If a man love me, he will keep my word: and my Father will love him, and we will come unto him, and make our abode with him' (John 14:23). Keeping Christ's word — that is the link between the love of the disciple and the love of the Father, which leads to that wonderful union in which the Father's love causes him to draw near to the loving heart and dwell in it. 'If ye keep my commandments, ye shall abide in my love; even as I have kept my Father's commandments, and abide in his love' (15:10).

'Whoso keepeth his word, in him hath the love of God been perfected' — love has done its perfect work and has brought the perfected fulfilment of its highest promise. Thank God! This is a life which can be found and lived on earth — loving God, obeying God, being loved by God, until his love has been perfected in us.

Chapter 12

To Love as Christ Loved

> *Beloved, if God so loved us, we also ought to love one another. No man hath beheld God at any time: if we love one another, God abideth in us, and his love is perfected in us.*
> (1 John 4:11–12)

We have seen that keeping Christ's word is the first mark of a soul which is being perfected in love. The way of obedience – the loving obedience of the perfect heart, the obedience of a life wholly given up to God's will – is the path into the presence and love of the Father, which the Son has opened up. It is the only path which leads into perfect love.

The commandments of Christ are all included in the one word 'love', because love is the fulfilment of the law. 'A new commandment I give unto you, that ye love one another; even as I have loved you, that ye also love one another' (John 13:34). This is Christ's word: the one who keeps this word keeps all the commandments. So love for one's brethren is the second mark of the soul which is seeking to enter the life of perfect love.

Because of the very nature of things it cannot be otherwise. 'Love seeketh not its own' (1 Cor. 13:5). Love loses itself in going out to live in others. Love is the death of self: where self still lives, there can be no possibility of perfect love. Love is the very being and glory of God. It is his nature and property as God to give from his own life to all his creatures, to share his own goodness and blessedness. In giving his Son he gave himself, to be the life and joy of man. When that love of God enters the heart it imparts its own nature, and the desire to give itself to the very death for others. When the heart wholly yields itself to be transformed into this nature and likeness, then love takes possession — there the love of God is perfected.

People often ask whether the term 'perfect love' refers to the love of God for us or our love for God. It refers to both. The love of God is One, as God is One; it is his life, his very being. When his love descends and enters a human heart, it retains its nature; it is the divine life-principle within us. God's love for us, our love for God and Christ, our love for our Christian brethren and for all men — all these are simply aspects of the same life of God. Just as there is one Holy Spirit, working through his diverse gifts, so there is one divine love, the love of the Spirit, which dwells in God and in us.

Understanding this is a wonderful help to our faith. It teaches us that we cannot love God or our brethren or our enemies by our own efforts. We can only do it if the divine love is dwelling in us. How well we do it depends upon how far we yield ourselves to the divine love as a living power within us, as a life which has been born into us and which the Holy Spirit strengthens. What we need to do first of all is to rest in God, to cease from effort, to know that he is in us, and to surrender to the love which lives and works in us in a power which is from above.

How well John must have remembered that night with Jesus when he spoke so wonderfully about love! How impossible it must have appeared to the disciples for them to truly love as he had loved! There had been so much pride, envy and selfishness among them — everything except love like his. They had even argued that night at the supper table. They could never love like the Master did — it was impossible.

But what a change was brought about when the Risen One breathed on them and said, 'Receive ye the Holy Ghost' (John 20:22)! And how that change was consummated when the Holy Spirit came down from heaven and filled their hearts with the love of God, drawing upon that wonderful love which was flowing in a holy interchange between the Father and the Son, now that they had met again in glory! In the love of the day of Pentecost perfect love celebrated its first great triumph in the hearts of men.

The love of God still reigns. The Spirit of God still waits to take possession of hearts in which he has as yet had too little room to work. He had been in the disciples all the time, but they had not understood this. He had entered into them on that evening when Jesus breathed on them. But it was

To Love as Christ Loved

at Pentecost that he filled them so that divine love prevailed and overflowed, and they were perfected in love.

Let our every effort to love and our every experience of how feeble our love is lead us and draw us on to Jesus on the Throne. In him the love of God is revealed and glorified and made accessible to us. Let us believe that the love of God can come down as a fire which will consume and destroy self. Let us love one another with a pure, fervent heart, because the Holy Spirit is in us, leading us on and preparing us, as he did the disciples, so that we may receive him in the fullness of power from above. This is the direct gift from the exalted Jesus to all who are ready to have God's love perfected in them. Let our hearts thirst and hope for nothing less than this.

Chapter 13

God Living in Us

> *No man hath beheld God at any time: if we love one another, God abideth in us, and his love is perfected in us: Hereby know we that we abide in him, and he in us, because he hath given us of his Spirit.*
>
> (1 John 4:12–13)

'No man hath beheld God at any time.' We are not yet able to have a direct vision of God. It is death to all created things; the all-consuming, all-absorbing fire of its glory is not compatible with our present earthly state. But instead we have been given an equivalent which can prepare and train us for the glorious vision, and which can also satisfy the soul by giving it as much of God as it can contain. We cannot look upon God, but we can have God living in us, and we can have his love perfected

God Living in Us

in us. Although the brightness of God's glory may not yet be seen, the presence of God's love — which is the very essence of that glory — may indeed be known.

And what is the way to this blessedness? God lives in us and his love perfected in us '*if we love one another*'. We may not see God, but we may instead look upon our brother in Christ. In him we have compensation for the loss of the vision of God. He will awaken and bring out the divine love within us; he will exercise and strengthen and develop it; he will draw down the divine love to do its beloved work through us, and so to perfect love within us. In my brother I have someone through whom God wants me to prove all my love for him. Through love for a brother, however unlovely he may be, love proves that self no longer lives; that it is a flame of the fire which consumed the Lamb of God himself; that it is God's love being perfected in me; that it is God himself living and loving within me.

'If we love one another, God abideth in us. Hereby know we that we abide him, and he in us, because he hath given us of his Spirit.' The wonderful knowledge that God lives in us and that his love is perfected in us is not the result of reflection or a deduction made from what we see in ourselves. No. The divine love and the divine indwelling are seen only in a divine light. We see them because God 'hath given us of his Spirit'. In his Gospel John records how little he and the other disciples understood the words of Jesus and how little they had experienced the truth of them, until that never-to-be-forgotten day of Pentecost when their understanding was illuminated in the light of the Fire which came from heaven. It is the Holy Spirit alone who makes Jesus permanently present to the soul which will rest content with nothing less — he does this not in his ordinary, gracious activity, such as that which the disciples had experienced before Pentecost, but in his special empowering, which comes directly from the Throne of the exalted Jesus. It is by the Holy Spirit alone that we know that God dwells in us and that we dwell in him and that his love is perfected in us.

As the Christian life was in the time of the disciples, so it is now. By slow steps we have to master now one side of the truth, then another, to practise now one grace and then a different one. It may be that for a time the Christian's whole heart is devoted to knowing and doing God's will. Then, later, he feels as if there is just one thing he has to do — to love; he feels that in his home, in all his dealings with people, in his outlook on the Church and the world, he needs only to practise love. After a time he becomes aware of how he is failing in this, and he turns to the word of God, which calls him to exercise faith, to give up self-effort and to trust in God, who causes him to want and to do his will. Once again he falls short, and he feels that there is only one thing which can meet his need — a share in the Pentecostal gift, a greater empowerment by the Spirit than he has ever had before.

None of us should be discouraged. Let us seek to obey, love and trust God with a perfect heart. Let us press on to perfection, confidently expecting that this word from God will be realised in our lives: 'If we love one another, God abideth in us, and the love of God is perfected in us. Hereby know we that we

God Living in Us

abide in him and he in us, because he hath given us of his Spirit.'

It is only in the path of love — love seeking to be perfect, expressed in practical ways — that we can experience the wonderful blessing of living in God and having him live in us. And it is only by the Holy Spirit that we can know that God lives in us and that his love is perfected in us. God is love, so it is certain that he longs to live in us, because love is the desire to communicate oneself and to get entire possession of the beloved one. God is love, and he sends the Spirit of his Son to fill the hearts which are open to him. A perfect heart can count upon being filled with perfect love. We should let nothing less than perfect love be our aim, so that we may have God living in us, and so that by the Holy Spirit which he has given us we may know that he lives in us.

Chapter 14

The Likeness of Christ

*Herein is love made perfect with us,
that we may have boldness in the day
of judgement; because as he is, even
so are we in this world.*

(1 John 4:17)

Let us look back on the steps in the life of perfect love which we have considered so far. The divine love, entering the heart, manifests itself first of all in loving obedience to Christ. An active love for the brethren becomes the chief mark and manifestation of that obedience. In this obedient love and loving obedience fellowship with God is developed and strengthened. The Holy Spirit gives the evidence and permanent assurance of this fellowship. So this is the path in which love is perfected: obedience to Christ; love for the brethren; God dwelling in us, and we in him; the communication and revelation

The Likeness of Christ

of all this by the Holy Spirit. All these are correlated ideas; they imply and condition one another. Together they make up the blessed life of perfect love.

The perfect heart began by wholeheartedly seeking God alone. It found him through the perfect way of obedient love for him and ministering love for the brethren. And so it came in Christ to the Father, and to fellowship with him. Thus it was prepared and opened up for that special illumination by the Spirit which revealed God's indwelling of the heart. Beginning as a little seed, the perfect heart has now grown up and borne fruit. It is now a heart in which the love of God is perfected. That love has taken full possession and reigns throughout the believer's whole being.

Is there anything more that can be said about perfect love? Yes, two things. First, let us think about the words, 'because *as he is*, even so are we in the world.' In Christ we are perfect. We have been made perfect with the same perfection as that with which Christ himself was perfected. Our place in Christ implies that we have a perfect likeness to his life and Spirit, to his disposition and character.

In chapter 2 John says, 'He that saith he abideth in him ought himself also to walk *even as he walked*' (verse 6). Likeness to Christ in his life of obedience on earth is the mark of perfect love.

In chapter 3 we read, 'Every one that hath this hope set on him purifieth himself, *even as he is pure*' (verse 3). In the coming glory we will see Christ as he is, and we will be like him. We now purify ourselves in order to be pure like Christ; this is the preparation for being like him when we see him as he is. Likeness to Christ's purity in this earthly life is a second mark of perfect love.

We also read in chapter 3, 'Hereby know we love, because he laid down his life for us: and we ought to lay down our lives for the brethren' (verse 16). Likeness to Christ in his love towards us is a third mark of perfect love.

On the last night Jesus prayed to the Father for us, 'that they may be one, even as we are one; I in them, and thou in me, that they may be perfected into one' (John 17:22-23). Likeness to Christ in his fellowship with the Father — God in us and we in him — is a fourth mark of perfect love.

God gave Christ to us in order that he should save us by becoming our life, by taking us up into union with himself. God could have no higher aim and could bestow no greater blessing upon us than seeing Christ in us: 'as he is, even so are we in the world.'

The second and final point about perfect love which we need to consider is suggested to us by the words, 'that we may have boldness in the day of judgement'. God has committed judgement to the Son, who is the perfected Son of Man. His judgement will be a spiritual one. He himself will be its standard; likeness to him will be what will qualify us to pass in and reign with him. Perfect love is perfect union and perfect likeness: we will have boldness on the day of judgment because we will be like him.

You seekers after perfection, it is in Christ that you will find what you seek. God's love is revealed in him. In him and his life you enter into that love, and it enters into you; in him love takes possession of you and transforms you into his likeness; in him

God comes to make his home in you; in him love is perfected. Jesus prayed 'that the love wherewith thou lovedst me may be in them, and I in them' (John 17:26). The love of God is perfected in us; we are perfected in love; we have boldness on the day of judgement, because as Christ is, even so are we.

Chapter 15

Waiting for God

*I wait the Lord, my soul doth wait,
And in his word do I hope.
My soul looketh for the Lord,
More than watchmen look for the morning.*
                              (Psalm 130:5–6)

With what intense longing the morning is often awaited — by a sailor in a shipwrecked vessel, by a traveller who has lost his way at night in a dangerous country, by an army which finds itself surrounded by an enemy. The morning light shows what hope and means of escape there may be. The morning may bring life and liberty.

Paul says, 'God [hath] shined in our hearts, to give the light of the knowledge of the glory of God in the face of Jesus Christ' (2 Cor. 4:6). Just as the sun shines its beautiful life-bringing light onto the earth, so God shines his light into our hearts, the

Waiting for God

light of his glory in Christ. Our hearts are meant to have that light filling them and gladdening them all the day. And they can have it, because God is a Sun — his love shines without ceasing.

If you are not experiencing this in your life, do not accept that state of affairs but say with the Psalmist, 'I wait for the Lord. My soul waits for the Lord more than watchmen watch for the morning.' Remember that the first thing the light does is to reveal the darkness. Look upon your awareness of your sin, your unrest and your powerlessness as proof that the light of God is arising in your heart. Do not be afraid to yield to that light. Be content to bow in humble penitence, in response to the measure of light which has been given to you. Be sure of this precious truth: the light which shows the darkness has also come to show the way out of it. Wait for the Lord.

The light expels the darkness. There is a divine power in the light of God. John says about our blessed Lord, 'In him was life; and the life was the light of men' (John 1:4). The light which God shines into your heart is nothing less than the outshining and the inshining of the divine life of the blessed Son. Just as the light of our sun works with silent but mighty energy at giving life to nature and making it beautiful, so the light which God gives works mightily in the heart, casting out the darkness and the evil, spreading its own blessed purity and brightness everywhere. Oh, wait for this more than the watchers wait for the morning! Pray, 'O God, shine into my heart! My soul waits for you.' It is God who must do it; it is God who will do it.

The light gives fellowship — fellowship with God,

who is light, fellowship with Christ, who is the Light of the World, and fellowship with all the children of the light. We know and love one another not in the light of human affection and compatibility, but in the light of God.

The light of God is love and joy and blessing. Just as the sun shines itself away unwearyingly, so the Son shone himself away to the point of death, so that the glory of God might shine into us and become the joy of our hearts. God's love, shed abroad by the Holy Spirit, is the light which fills our whole being. Wait for the Lord, until his light has completely filled you.

In the light we can walk and work. As we walk in the light we become children of the light completely. We let our light, the light of God, shine, so that men may see our good works and glorify our Father in heaven. Gently, silently, lovingly, unceasingly, we give ourselves to reflect the light and love which God so constantly shines into us. Our one task in life is to wait for and admit and then transmit the light of God in Christ.

Christian, do not rest until you know the full, unbroken shining of God in your heart. To this end, yield to every stirring of the light which shows you some as yet unconquered evil in your life. Just bring it to the light; let the light shine upon it and shine it out of you. Count upon it that God wants to fill you with the light of his glory. Wait for the Lord — wait for him more than watchmen wait for the morning.

Chapter 16

Humility, the Glory of the Creature

They shall cast their crowns before the throne, saying, 'Worthy art thou, our Lord and our God, to receive the glory and the honour and the power: for thou didst create all things, and because of thy will they were, and were created.

(Revelation 4:11)

When God created the universe it was with the one object of making his creations partakers of his perfection and blessedness, and of displaying in them the glory of his love and wisdom and power. God wished to reveal himself in and through created beings by communicating to them as much of his own goodness and glory as they were capable of receiving. But this was not a giving to the creature of something which it could possess by itself, a certain life or goodness of which it had charge and control. By no means. Because God is the ever-living, ever-present, ever-active One, who upholds all things by the word of his power and in whom all things exist, the relation of the creature to God could only be one of unceasing, absolute, universal dependence. Just as God by his power once created, so by that same power God must at every moment maintain. The life which God bestows is imparted not once for all, but every moment by the constant activity of his mighty power. The creature has not only to look back to the origin and first beginning of existence, and acknowledge that it owes everything to God but it must also now, at every moment, present itself as an empty vessel in which God can dwell and manifest his power and goodness. This attitude of humility, of entire dependence upon God, is from the very nature of things the first duty and the only happiness of the creature. It is its highest virtue — indeed, it is the root of its every virtue.

So it follows that pride, or the loss of this humility, is the root of every sin and evil. It was when the now-fallen angels began to look upon themselves with complacency that they were led to disobedience, and so were cast down from the light of heaven into outer darkness. The same thing happened when the serpent breathed the poison of his pride, the desire to be like God, into the hearts of our first parents, so that they too fell from their high estate into all the wretchedness in which man is now sunk. In heaven and earth pride or self-exaltation is the gate and the birth of hell.

So it follows that we can only be redeemed by the

Humility, the Glory of the Creature

restoration of the lost humility, of the original and only true attitude of the creature to its God. And so Jesus came to bring humility back to earth, to make us partakers of it, and through it to save us. He humbled himself in becoming a man. The humility which we see in him first possessed him in heaven; it brought him from there to here, and he brought it. Here on earth 'he humbled himself, becoming obedient even unto death' (Phil. 2:8). His humility gave his death its value, and so became our redemption. And now the salvation which he gives to us is nothing less and nothing other than a sharing of his own life and death, his own character and spirit, his own humility, which is the ground and root of his relation to God and of his redeeming work. Jesus Christ took and filled the place and destiny of the creature, man, by his life of perfect humility. His humility is our salvation; his salvation is our humility.

And so the lives of the saints or saved ones must bear the stamp of deliverance from sin and full restoration to the original state of man: their relation to God and to their fellow men must be marked by an all-pervading humility. Without this they cannot have a lasting, consistent experience of God's presence and favour and of the power of his Spirit. Without humility there can be no abiding faith, love, joy or strength. Humility is the only soil in which the graces take root; a lack of humility is a sure explanation of every defect and failure in the Christian's life. Humility is not a grace or virtue like all the others; rather, it is the foundation for all of them, because it alone ensures a right attitude to God and allows him to do his will.

God has created us as intelligent beings in such a way that the clearer our understanding of the real nature or the absolute need of a command is, the more ready and full will be our obedience to that command. God's call to humility has been so neglected in the Church because the true nature of humility has been too little understood. It is not something which we bring to God or which he bestows upon us. Rather, it is simply the sense of nothingness which comes to us when we truly see that God is all, and which causes us to make way for God to be all in our lives. We then consent to be the vessel in which the life and the glory of God are to work and manifest themselves, and surrender our whole selves – will, mind, body and emotions – to the Lord. Humility is our true nobility as God's creatures. It is simply an acknowledgement of the truth that we are creatures, and a yielding to God so that he may take his rightful place in us.

Humility ought to be the chief mark of the uprightness of earnest Christians, of those who pursue and profess holiness. It is often said that this humility is lacking. One reason for this lack may be that in the teaching of the Church humility has never had the position of supreme importance which rightly belongs to it. And again, this oversight may be due to the neglect of the truth that, although sin is indeed a strong motivation to humility, there is one of even wider and mightier influence. It makes even Jesus, the angels and the holiest saints in heaven humble. It is the knowledge that the first and chief mark of the relation of the creature to the Creator and the secret of his blessedness is the humility and nothingness which leaves God free to be all.

Chapter 17

A New Year Meditation

And the Lord said unto Abram, after that Lot was separated from him, 'Lift up now thine eyes, and look from the place where thou art, northward and southward and eastward and westward: For all the land which thou seest, to thee will I give it, and to thy seed for ever . . . Arise, walk through the land in the length of it and in the breadth of it; for unto thee will I give it.'

(Genesis 13:14–15, 17)

Abram had parted from Lot. In allowing Lot to go his separate way, he had proved his faith — he had shown that he believed that he was rich in possessing God and his promise. His separation from his kindred was now complete; he was now entirely free to listen to God alone. He was entering upon a new stage in his pilgrim life, and God at once met him with a renewal of his promise. God came and spoke to him again; he called him to look upon the land which had been promised and which would be given to him.

How many of us are longing and praying that the New Year may be a new beginning? How many sad hearts will make a vow of renewed consecration to God and will pray for a new revelation of God as January arrives? In order to understand what such a recommitment really means, we need to take in the lesson which this new beginning in Abram's life teaches us.

'And the Lord said unto Abram . . .' When we give ourselves afresh to God, let it be our first thought to listen for him coming to us and telling us what he wants us to say and do. *Have open ears for God's voice*. Do not imagine that because you are separated to God you now know how to serve him. I am deeply persuaded that the chief reason for the failure and feebleness of so many Christians is that they so seldom keep their ears open, waiting for God's voice and teaching, for the guidance of his Holy Spirit.

The very first effect of a true consecration to God ought to be the deep sense that now God himself alone may say what we are to do. Out of this will grow a true confession of ignorance and a great assurance that God will not withhold the needed guidance. Again, this will lead to a very humble and dependent waiting for the teaching which is hidden from the wise and intelligent, which flesh and blood cannot give, which comes only by revelation from the Father.

What was it that the Lord said to Abram after he and Lot had parted? 'Lift up now thine eyes, and look from the place where thou art, northward and

A New Year Meditation

southward and eastward and westward: For all the land which thou seest, to thee will I give it.' If open ears is the first mark of a consecrated soul, *open eyes* is the second. When God first called Abram, it was to 'the land that *I will show thee*' (Gen. 12:1). He had to go out in faith, not knowing where he was going. He did not know a single step of the way. There are times in the spiritual life when we have to believe in what appears dark and utterly beyond our comprehension. Then comes another stage, when we receive the command to look up and gaze, and see in every direction over all the extent of the Land of Promise – to take in all that God has told us about his plan and his pleasure. Christian, once you have heard God speak out his thoughts to you, make them your own by contemplation. 'Lift up thine eyes and look' until the vision of all that there is in Christ, in the Word, in God's plan, in the world – all that is waiting for God's people to take possession – has passed before the eyes of your soul, and has entered in and filled it.

Then comes the third need of the consecrated soul. As well as opened eyes and listening ears there must also be *willing feet*: 'Arise, walk through the land.' The contemplative side of the Christian life is of no value if it does not prepare the believer for the active side. It is only in action, in *doing* the will of God, that the great salvation which he has given us becomes a reality in our lives. 'Lift up thine eyes and look' is only the prelude to 'Arise and walk.' Both are equally needed. It is only as the Holy Spirit opens our eyes and reveals what the redemption in Christ means that we can really see where God wants to take us. But even this is not all that is needed. There is still another side to the truth. Only through a willing, ready obedience, only by rising and walking, by carrying out God's commands in everything, can we personally appropriate and realise the salvation which has been achieved by Christ and revealed by the Spirit.

Christian, listen carefully for God's voice speaking to you. Look hard and long at everything God shows you. And then arise and walk through the length and breadth of the land. Only in this way will you have the fulfilment of the promise, 'unto thee will I give it.' Only in this way can your faith be perfected — only if you have your ears opened to hear the secret voice, your eyes anointed to see God's wonderful things, your feet prepared to walk wherever he wants you to go.

May God give us all such an outlook on the coming year and on God's wonderful grace for us in it. May each consecrated believer hear God's voice renewing his promises and teaching his will. May each of us catch the meaning of the command, 'From the place where thou art' — where your God has met you — 'lift up thine eyes and look.' And may each of us with joyful swiftness obey the call to 'Arise, and walk through the land.'

To everyone reading these lines I offer my New Year greetings, with a prayer that the blessing which Abram knew may be theirs at the start of the year and all the way through it: God meeting them and speaking to them; God teaching them to lift up their eyes and look, to arise and walk; God confirming and fulfilling his promise that 'the land which thou seest, to thee will I give it.'

The African Evangelical Fellowship

The African Evangelical Fellowship is an international evangelical mission. This book is published in association with them. It had its beginnings in the challenge of missionary outreach in South Africa in the 1880s. Together with Spencer Walton, Andrew Murray was God's man to accept this challenge and the work of the South African General Mission began in Capetown in 1889. Andrew Murray was the president of the S.A.G.B. until his death in 1917. Since then, over 1300 missionaries have served in 13 different countries of Southern Africa under the S.A.G. and A.E.F., as the mission has been known since 1961. Today over 360 missionaries are still active in Africa serving with those churches established under past ministries. For more information about their work, please contact them at their International Office, 35 Kingfisher Court, Hambridge Road, Newbury, Berkshire RG14 5SJ, England.

Other AEF offices are:-

Australia
PO Box 292
Castle Hill
New South Wales 2154

Canada
470 McNicoll Avenue
Willowdale
Ontario M2H 2E1

USA
PO Box 2896
Boone
North Carolina 28607

United Kingdom
30 Lingfield Road
Wimbledon
London SW19 4PU

Zimbabwe
99 Gaydon Road
Graystone Park
Borrowdale
Harare

South Africa
Rowland House
6 Montrose Avenue
Claremont 7700

New Zealand
PO Box 1390
Invercargill

Europe
5 Rue de Meautry
94500 Champigny-sur-Marne
France